Rodent Angel

Poems

Debra Weinstein

New York University Press
New York and London

811.54
Wei

Grateful acknowledgement is made to the following publications where some of these poems first appeared:

The American Poetry Review, The American Voice, Bastard Review, The Brooklyn Review, Common Lives/Lesbian Lives, Critical Matrix, The Family Next Door, 5 am, Global City Review, Hurricane Alice, The James White Review, New Myths/MSS, Outweek, The Portable Lower East Side, and *Tikkun* and *The New Fuck You-Adventures in Lesbian Reading,* edited by Eileen Myles and Liz Kotz, Semiotext(e) 95, New York.

The author wishes to thank the National Endowment for the Arts, The MacDowell Colony, and The Corporation of Yaddo for generous support which made this book possible.

Library of Congress Cataloging-in-Publication Data
Weinstein, Debra
    Rodent angel : poems / Debra Weinstein.
       p.   cm.
    ISBN 0-8147-9308-8 (cloth : alk. paper). — ISBN 0-8147-9307-X (pbk. : alk. paper)
     I. Title.
PS3573.E39648R63   1996
811'.54—dc20   95-52194
                           CIP

New York University Press books are printed on acid-free paper, and their binding materials are chosen for strength and durability.

Rodent Angel

ELMER HOLMES BOBST AWARDS FOR EMERGING WRITERS

Established in 1983, the Elmer Holmes Bobst Awards in Arts and Letters are presented each year to individuals who have brought true distinction to the American literary scene. Recipients of the Awards include writers as varied as Toni Morrison, John Updike, Russell Baker, Eudora Welty, Edward Albee, Arthur Miller, Joyce Carol Oates, and James Merrill. The Awards were recently expanded to include categories devoted to emerging writers of fiction and poetry, and in 1995 the jurors selected winners in each category, Lori Baker for her short stories, *Crazy Water: Six Fictions* and Don Judson for his novella, *Bird-Self Accumulated,* and Debra Weinstein for her collection of poems, *Rodent Angel.*

For Deborah and for Gabrielle—

"Very many are living and are remembering that family living can go on existing." —GERTRUDE STEIN

"For something is amiss or out of place when mice with wings can wear a human face." —THEODORE ROETHKE

CONTENTS

2. In the Year of My Grandfather

3. The Rat's Face Haunted Me

4. *The Story of Life*

5. *Postscript*

Rodent Angel

1. In the Year
of the
Small Birds

Onanism

She was for masturbation,
for getting to know yourself,
sexually. She caressed
her leg as she spoke. She sensed

unresolved conflict, Oedipal
strivings. Her own daughter,
she said, would walk
naked in her bra, try to take
her place in bed. This was nothing

to cry about. Every girl
wanted what mother had, wanted
her mother. She had my parents
in analysis and group. I would hear

her muffled name
through their door, as I lay
in bed, making
the first tentative gestures
toward myself, touching
thighs, hair. A woman

might do this with waxed
fruit, the back
of a hairbrush, a long
silver object borrowed
from a husband. One inserted the walking
stick; spilled

herself, fucked its antique
head. Fucked
the monogrammed head
of the father. Left to her own

devices, one straddled
a vacuum cleaner, enticed
a puppy, led
the warm animal tongue
to her lap. Long ago
I imagined myself
conceived in masturbation.
My father handing
the great white seed
to my mother, who took it
on her fingertip,
and placed it delicately
inside her body.

Collusion

Even when saccharine
was removed from the stores,
you continued to serve it.
You bought it on sale,
in large quantities.
And I remember him rising
from the basement, coming
to that table, spooning
the sweet white powder
into his coffee. He was the rat

poisoned over time.
He grew tumors on the soft
parts of his hands. Inside
he grew a limp balloon. You fed
him sugar-free jello and left trays
of dietetic candy in every room.
You called him "squirrel."

Twilight

A man puts a doll's
head in a vice, turns the lever.
Her name is Talky Tina and
she hates him, wants
to kill him. He tightens
the grip, but the cheeks
don't puff. "Don't talk,"

you say and turn me over.
You hold my legs perfectly
still. I hate you, I'll kill
you, I want
to say, but I bite
my tongue.

It is twilight,
and something ought
to smile down, the mirror
or the moon.

The Fiction Writer

He touches himself
absently. In his hand,
his thinning hair.

All day he sits at the window,
tapping his eraser. He mumbles,
"Beth, his first woman,
wanted children. Her soul,
clear . . ."

When he looks at me
he sees hair on the soap,
a loose toothpaste cap. He knows
a woman Fidel Castro
invited to Cuba. Another
with two children and
a prison record. Once
he lived with a potter.

He sits on the edge
of the twin bed; distant,
indifferent. He watches
me make love to a woman.

Rodent Angel

This morning a dead
rat on my path—bloated,
wet, its bowels
worm-like
shit below the body.
How do we approach the dead?
I wanted to call someone.
The sanitation man
loading garbage
into the belly of his truck.
My sister,
the policewoman, riding
her black horse
high above the childhood city.

I sat mute on my haunches.
I saw the rat carcasses
on Weiming Road; the man
with his bags of poison. I saw them
in the history museum behind
glass, imported
from Africa, Madrid; blind
in both eyes, stuffed
with cotton. Nameless rats
with lips sewn back—
I saw my mother's father
in the satin box. He had the sweet
face of a man asleep
after a heavy meal;

of the pedophile,
sleeping with a child's
hand between his thighs.

The eyes are stunned open.
It never occurred
to me to touch him, to lean
over to say goodbye. My mother
swept the hair from his face,
then leaned over to kiss him.
He was more beautiful this way.
Death had softened his mouth,
stilled his hands.

The Pact

Each morning
exfoliating the dead
skin cells, she glances
out the window.
Electromagnetic waves
reflect off the car and it shines.
Her lines deepen. When
I sleep in her white
bed, under the flowering dog-
wood, under the Navaho
EKG, and brass
canopy, I touch myself.

In her birthmark, I see
naked girls. They run together
in a field or disrobe
in the raftered hall.
They touch small plum
breasts, then lie red-faced
on the floor. Air pushes

through the curtain. She lights
a match, says,
"I am your nightmare,"
then touches my face.
Outside men
scale trees in black
suits fixing
the power lines.

The Seduction of a Younger Woman by an Older One

I sit on the chaise
lounge holding
the portable phone. Reflection
bores me. I wade through cold
water, come
up from behind, and lay
a wet palm on her external
oblique. It is smooth, firm,
and I reach up, touch her breasts.
They feel like small summer
fruit, exotic, cool, and I turn her around,
force her down, grab
her legs. I hold her
like a wheelbarrow, split
open. I raise
and lower her. Water spills
from her hair. I want
to eat from her mouth. I want
her milky, swollen. It is August,

and the lines
are down. Men
in the trees. The young
birch is tied to the fence
so it will grow
straight. Once I promised never
to seduce her. Now
I lift her onto the blue
edge and begin.

HIV

I feared their blood,
their poisoned cells
infecting my cells. The old lovers
returning by fluorescent
assay. My blood
making the antibodies. I feared
spit, bodily fluids. The aerospace man

I made while the big
blue head of Johnny Carson
played. I feared
his bedroom suite. And another
I made on a bed of dirty
laundry. I touched his red, shaved
skull, and later he showed me
his Nixon pins. I feared

needles. A man I knew
for an hour. The former high school
sweetheart, ever hopeful, turning
in the railroad flat to say, "I want
to want women." I feared my first
woman who slept with a woman
who slept with a man who held a gun
to her head; she was
mysteriously coughing
in the dark. I feared

the sleeping girl,
the girl who needed sperm
to sleep, and the lover
she let enter her double bed,
cock first. I feared the couple
who never kissed, the pills
they took, their anal
sex. I feared my blood
in its vial, numbered
and sealed.

Infant Fingers

"When you were a baby,"
my mother said, "you had
the most beautiful fingers.
I would sit and admire them
for hours. Your fingers

were like the pink, shrivelled
fingers of the newborn mole
which guide it
through tunnels
underground. The mole's hands

are like infant's
hands, stuck
to a rodent's body."

Suzanne

My mother loved her baby
carriage, a huge metal boat
that rocked on a rusty spring. She left me
on the driveway with the newborn
asleep with the pink
lace band *Suzanne Rebecca* across
the top. I remember fearing
it would coast down Broadview Drive
with me in tow, fearing
the squirrel who would
climb into a carriage and suck
a baby's face
for milk. Once, I let Suzanne glide
down a neighbor's driveway
and smash into a rock.

Years later, I knocked Suzanne
to the ground for asking me to fix
her scissors. She rose
in confusion with pain
around her mouth and eyes
before she cried. I held her
to me, crushing her against
my body, saying
I was sorry, the way my father
did after he beat me once
for locking the bathroom door.

Often Suzanne
would climb
into my bed and sleep
her last ten minutes pressing
her wet bottom against me.

Linda

My sister loved her plastic
Linda with furrowed
skull and blinking
eyes; rocked
her in the cradle
with the cracked butterfly
motif and stained
foam mattress my father
cut in the basement
with a razor. How many mornings

I found Suzanne's cold bottom
in my bed, her doll's pointed
hand in my face; or turning,
smacked my head
against the doll's brainless
head, and cried. That summer

we took Linda to the beach, and
she floated belly-up. We held her
one hand each, and lifted
her above the waves. After swimming
Suzanne shook Linda,
then cried, scratching
the rusted eyelids.

In the home movie, Suzanne
runs on the beach. A phantom
arm comes in from the left

and smacks her. She drops
the doll and falls to the sand.
She turns to the camera, pleading.

Later my brother entered
her room with wirecutters
and snapped the fingers
off her Linda, and left
them on the radiator.

All that is severed remains.

Route One

There are girls you cannot protect.
Running on the cover of the *Daily News*.
Running on the highway of South Vietnam.
I tried to protect my brother holding
his hand while my sister ran.
But there were fields on fire.
Water can burn you.
Clothes can burn you.
Touch, longed for, requited, can burn you.

Nixon spoke.
The war at the dinner table.
I saw soldiers in their hell pits,
a man shot in the head.
I saw the sprouts
of hair which grew in the crack
and spread outward.
The girl exposed me to myself.
I wanted to turn her face down
and run. I wanted to hide
her shame, but she was everywhere.
Running in the jellied gasoline, defoliated.
They had torn off her clothes
and sent her on this journey.

In the Year of the Small Birds

My father stood
on the ladder with his leather
glove and reached back
up under the eaves and brought
forth squirrels the size
of a child's finger,
with veined skulls and
eyes glued shut, and dropped
them into a basket. Sometimes
a squirrel would slip
and fall and lie thrashing
on the pavement. I often found
small birds under my window
in spring when my father
cleared the gutters. That year

my parents smelled
my grandfather's hands on me
and would not touch me.

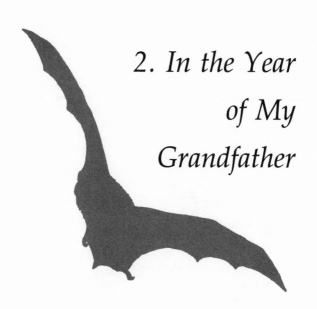

2. In the Year
of My
Grandfather

Jism

For that I never knew you,
I only learned to dread you.
I killed you with spermicide
I swallowed you whole.

There interposed a Fly—
between the sperm and me.
I slicked the cap with jelly,
applied the second skin. Because
I knew you and dreaded you,
I forced rhythm on you.

In the backseat
of my father's car,
learning to hand-jive.
In my platonic
first marriage,
the whole, barren,
gummy yearning
all night long. I never thought
to husband jism.

Once I kept jism
a coin in my purse.
Later, on ice
in the lab. Now
I must pay
for what once came

for free. O my
Homunculus,
I am ill.

The Garden

He draws seeds from
flowers. He makes them
disappear. Observe

my grandfather. He crushes
marigolds. He smears
an orange and gold sunset
underfoot.

Men tower above me.
Commit their crimes and go
unpunished. He grips me

like a wand. In the August
garden, he spills black seeds.

M.

A baby named for my grandfather
feeds in a dark room. I feed
the mother. My grandfather,
the pedophile, would have loved
this scene, painted
us naked, baby
between us. But art

imitates nothing.
We sit in a room of painted
flowers, and she fears
what I might do
alone with her child.
She's heard statistics.
Has seen a woman bite
her baby's cunt, then look up,
flushed with pleasure.

She says, "The victim and
the victimizer walk
hand in hand. I've
seen them in the park."

In the Year of My Grandfather

There were pails
in the kitchen.
There were access holes.
There was a strange scratching
in the attic above
my bedroom. When my father
came in with his ladder,
I couldn't tell
him about the hand
in my lap and the lap
that drew my hand into it. That summer

my father pulled
a nest out of the eaves, and I lay
in bed each night
wondering when
they would come for me: the rabid
family chewing through
the door, the ceiling. They moved
above me on pointed toes.
They would bite my face
and hands, gnaw
my fingers at the joints,
and I would be shot
nineteen times below
the stomach and vomit
blood. I would take
the needle every week,
that would touch my spine.

The mother squirrel
returned from foraging
and found the nest broken, the babies
gone. She heard their distant
bird-like squeaks. She stood
on the roof, on two hind
feet, her lips pulled
back, her teeth

exposed, like my mother
who stopped her car
on West Walnut Street and said,
"Don't tell me this. No."

Grief

Grief pierces my lip
and threads itself
through my tongue and
pulls my lip
with its fish-weight.

Love loosens my limbs and I tremble.

The Oath

I make an oath on a tissue
box. I promise to protect
the group, never to write
of my affair with a group
member. I come
individually on Wednesday
nights. We talk
about my mother. How
she shamed me
during childhood,

locked me out
of the house. "Treated
me like a dog," I say,
without feeling. The therapist
looks over her troubled
glasses. She is going
grey and hiding
it. She has come
to love me and lost
objectivity. She has served
as courier, go-between.
Has delivered me
my underwear, robe. Says,

"Let's talk about
the dog." But I feel
edgy, uncertain. Outside men
are rolling back

her pool cover, exposing
the black, filmy water. They
pour in chemicals, shout, "Mother-
fucker." She turns on
the white noise, then leans
back, twiddles her bright,
painted thumbs. Words

catch in my throat. Mother-
fuck-her. I see socks,
dirty laundry, my former lover,
the woman in group, turning
me out, refusing
to speak. I hear
the rationale, the group's
assent; and my own
mouth, agreeing
to anything. The therapist
stands up, opens
her freckled arms, and the universe
of loss enlarges
to take in one more.

Wuhan Station

That evening we took a bath
and held each other in bed
a little longer. When the last,
slant of your face was gone, I was a train
travelling north China alone.

I want civil endings: let no lover ever leave me
at Wuhan Station in Hubei Province on a night
full of red neon and chaos, with bells and
chickens and no English, wishing me
love and good luck.

Mei Gue

(Chinese for *beautiful country; America*)

Looking to relieve myself, I find
the community ditch where you squat
one leg on either side
of the irrigation canal. I am finally
unzipped and balanced.
There is a small, tight
feeling in my lower region.
There are four Chinese
women looking in. They have come
to see my Mei Gue, my beautiful

country, my foreign
body with its American
vagina. Piss falling
against the stream
makes a flat sound. A woman
undresses, squats
besides me and looks.

I am America: the white crotch
bringing forth the fertile
waste; the dark
hiding the hooded crown.

Mother Eye

You said, "a woman loves her child more than her husband." You did not say "I."

Poison

Above my room
the mother squirrel
turned her teats
to the newborn rodents,
and nursed them
with her poisoned milk.
They walked dizzily
across the patio. They suckled
their mother's carcass.
They stared ahead
with big, black eyes.

Who would shut the eyes
of the dead, newborn squirrels?

Not their mother,
who lay on her side
with her mouth agape.

Not my mother who snapped
back the red curtain,
who felt the bile
rise up in her throat.

She nursed her newborn daughter,
then drank black coffee
to wash away
the taste of poison.

In the Museum of the Deformed Deer

1

I saw the cross-eyed
baby deer. I saw
a deer without eyelids
glued to a plaque. I read

of the hunter
waiting for the one-legged
deer to crawl out
on its belly, dragging
its foot in the dirt.

2

Once I met the halogen
eye of the plastic
surgeon, and lay twisted
on the table; my bones
exposed, my skin
sewn back. And my mother

stroked the mold
of my face
on the counter, and said
I was beautiful.

In the Year of the Live Birth

My father reached
into the rodent hole
and brought me forth. He pulled
my slippery flesh
from the dark; then we stood
eye to eye. At his side

was the shovel
with its flattened blade.
There were others
clubbed to death or eaten
with placental membranes.
He looked upon me with compassion.

My Grandfather

My grandfather, eighteen
years dead, once dropped
from the sky. I tried—
but I could not make a rat
an angel.

3. The Rat's Face Haunted Me

The Smallest Pebble

I am sick of the dead
immemorial, buried
and embalmed for life,
provided with eternal care.

I placed the smallest pebble
on my grandfather's grave,
not to say hello,
but to remind myself
there are limits to giving.

The Rat's Face Haunted Me

I had learned to stop
the rats
from coming. I resisted

the easy poem
with its gratuitous
violence and vilification
of the dead. I tried

to prevent
the flashbacks. But the rat's
face haunted me.
It was so ugly and pained.

It stared at its entrails
covered with flies.
It stared at the guts
piled neatly on its stomach.

It was the face
of an animal
beaten in the pasture,
of an old man
in ecstacy.

In the Year of the Stopped Car

The year of the infestation,
my grandfather exposed
the metal tooth
underneath his pants, and I ran
between the car

and the wall. That summer
my father buried
the baby squirrels alive,
throwing dirt in their mouths
and eyes, flattening the grave
with his tiny shovel; my mother
sat with her coffee and stared
out the window. And God

ate his way through
the attic door, came
to me on pointed toes—
and said he wanted
to father me, to feed me
food from the plastic
trays—and he told me
to eat poison.

"A woman loves her child
more than her husband."
My mother sat me on the queen-
sized bed. "Let's keep
this our secret," she said.

She had a smooth voice,
hoarse from cigarettes
and lies. She had stopped
her car on West Walnut Street
and turned, and seen
her daughter for the first time:
the long, pointed silhouette,
the growing teeth. My mother
fell into her sister's
arms, and wept—
The love of fathers
is queer. They take you
from the midwife's arms.
They bathe you in the silver
tub, they touch your thigh.
They live in the cellar,
below the house, and move
subterranean, beneath you. That summer

they hung the poison bells,
and my mother snapped back
the red curtain,
and saw the dead
squirrels. They lay
in groups of five. Huge, furry
mothers huddled
with their infant dead. She saw
the ashen babies,
almost black; and the pink face

of the newborn,
furless, with veins
at the surface, black
glass eyes, like her own.
It pushed aside
an infant corpse, and crawled
into its mother's arms.

Boots

I stand on the rug
in the off-white room. Below
me is a woman, naked,
unashamed. For I have gone
to the closet to put on
my boots, and asked
her to remain on all
fours. I am the rancher

walking circles, examining
her angles, spreading
her thighs. I have carried

this woman from the pool
to the kitchen, then over
the threshold, to the living
room. I have towelled
her dry on the circular
couch and held her. She smelled
like the dark, chlorinated, blue pools
of childhood, and my lungs
hurt, remembering. I could not

swim, and water filled
my mouth and eyes. I could
not fight. The sound of water
is like a woman's breath. The tip

of my boot is pointed,
sincere; and she's my horse,
my girl. I rub
her crotch with the embroidered
shoe. She winces,
she bucks.

A Little Death

When the first woman
lifted me to the blue
edge of the swimming
pool and parted

the wet strands
of pubic hair and kissed
my clitoris
with the tip
of her tongue, I was talking

about Jesus,
how he raised up
the whore, saying, "Oh God,

oh yes." She was stroking
my vagina with the flat
of her tongue. She had fingers
inside me. And Jesus

touched the blind girl's
eyes and gave her sight—
I shut my mouth, and lifted
up my pelvis—

Under Sea

In the Atlantic Ocean she found
the animals sensitive
to light, vibration, and touch.
The plume worm blossoms
sucking themselves in
when a hand passed over.

In bed it was a different
story. She would find the worm
and its tentacles and pull
them out one long sea
thread at a time.

The Berries

Your breasts
are like branches
weighed down
with berries.

Your breasts
float on the water.

I love to watch you
gathering berries.

I love you
naked in the fire
pond, eating
blueberries.

Each breast
above the water,
crowned
with a berry.

Last Night

> I dreamed that
> you and I had
> words. I dreamed
>
> I threw you
> in the pool. Your dress
> rose to the surface.
>
> Lightning cracked
> the sky. You offered
> me your hand
> and I accepted.
>
> Then I was tangled
> in your dress
> and pinned.
>
> Then I was riding
> my black horse
> to your door.
>
> Only the path
> was concealed
> from me. And you
> were a stranger
> asking directions.

First Love

He was a member of the Adolescent Group.
    She was a member of the Tuesday Night Group.
Was it love or infatuation?
    Was it love or repetition?
The therapist sat on her swivel
chair in the classroom
of the abandoned
high school.
    The therapist sat on her swivel
    chair in the office
    of her converted
    rec room.
There was intimacy and the hope for intimacy.
    There was intimacy and the fear of intimacy.
There was alcoholism and bottled rage.
    There was incest and the fear of men.
He sat across from the therapist.
    She sat at the therapist's shoulder.
I wanted him and it was acting out.
    I wanted her and it was criminal.

Homage to the Drum

I want to be beaten
with quick, short strokes,
with a wooden stick,
with an open hand.

This is my hide
from the animal kingdom.
I want to be beaten.

This is my bring forth
the belly whoop.
Beat me in measured time.

I am the life force.
Beat me for the elders.

I am the excitable spirit.
Beat me for the tribe.

I am whipped up and writhing.
Beat me immortal.

The Massage

I was shocked into solitude.
I was shocked by the woman's
hand under my ribcage
smoothing my knot.

This is my little pond
losing its water and this
is my love knot,
grief knot, knot
of my childhood.
This is my parent knot,
hard and unyielding.

I will not
I will not
I will not
grieve, love, give.

The City Rat

Splayed on the sidewalk,
the city rat.
I meant to get down on my knees.
But there were legions
of walkers down Seventh Avenue.
There was morning traffic.
And I could not understand
Psalm 46—the beasts
that perish, the beasts
that persist.

I was sickened by the kiss
of the angel, KS.
I was revolted unto death.
Forever and forever and forever—
the blue shoe-leather
of his thighs, his shut
left eye.

The bowels hung
in bloody ribbons
at the mouth and anus—
discharged like excrement,
sweat. A body says
goodbye in advance,
expels itself first.

The Alphabet

1

There is the alphabet of hope
and the alphabet of despair.

The alphabet of despair
with its three-letter diseases.

The alphabet of hope
with its three-letter cures.

2

The alphabet of despair
led me to a man
toxic to himself, poisoned
by his body. A man

with HIV fearing
CMV. With PCP fearing
MAI. A man reciting
the alphabet
like a prayer: AZT, ddI,
ddC. A man

in despair of AZT.
With thinning hair
and cheeks, fearing
flowers, unwashed fruit.

He has bright purple
lesions, a white
tongue of hair.

3

This poem is for John Maresca,
with his box of leather goods
and sequined dresses—
forever mingling hope and despair.

He got the MFA,
the mother fucking AIDS.

The Undertakers

I have given my face
to the plastic surgeons,
and my body to the internist,
and my mind to the analyst,
and my crotch to the doctor
with his metal instruments.

I have given them my female
troubles, my human troubles,
the white scar
of my childhood, my uterus,
protracted and tilted
back, and my first born
siphoned into a jar.

I have given them my skin,
my blood, my brains.
I have given them my rat
to probe and examine.

I have given my rat
to the decorated
men and women of science.

She rages and grinds.
She reproduces
five hundred thousand times.

She is meat
for the undertakers.

They split me open
and begin the dissection.

Prayer

for John Gabriel Maresca, Jr. (1964–1992)

He brought us into his house
and gave us shelter.

Gay men.

And he sat in our garden
like a king in paradise.

Who can forget the body
of the host pinned to the cross
or the helmet of the leatherman
he nailed to his wall.

Gay men.

Whoever embraces love
embraces his flesh
and the body of his lovers
and his drag-queen friends.

Grant this man peace
and entry into your kingdom—
for the fathers, the sons, and the ghosts—
holy, holy, holy—

Bless the homosexual.

Gay men.

The Dream of Rat

This is the rat
of impending motherhood.
This is the dream
of rat and the dream
of sexual intercourse.

She moves with the fragrant
grace of coming.
She is impaled on a throne.

With clawing, digging,
she burrows into
a nest of her making.

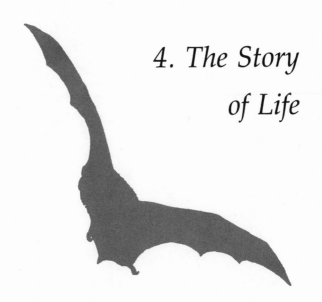

4. The Story
of Life

Goddess of the tubes and hoses,
I am a simple woman
who has walked from Chelsea.
I want to bring forth
the good within me, but fear
you will hurt me in my offering.
I have touched the sores
of a dying man, fearing the body.
I have wanted
to draw him into my breast,
but could not.
This is the prenatal test
routinely given before conception.
I offer my inside elbow to you.
I give you my blood.
I take the mortality test.
I am all men, mortal.
I am all women, immortal.

Storage Tank

You house my children
and my children's children.
You are the ship carrying descendent cargo.

You are shrouded in hazardous vapor
like a myth. You hold the ten prong
hanger dangling matter. The one
called back from eternity.

You have been cast off and delivered—
shipped to an office building,
and retrieved in my bedroom.

I do not know what it is like
to awaken suddenly, carried
in the body of another.

Blessing

Goddess of the basal body, bless us.
Goddess of the reproductive technology,
bless us with the storage tank of #517
at our bedside. Bless the lovers
whose love yields only love.
Make them a daughter, a son.
Bless them in perpetuity.

The Story of Life

*

These are the enzymes of the gods.
And this is their piss cup.
This is the dropper stuffed with cotton
that transports me back to matter.
I have made love and know
the principles of desire.
I have been love's chemist
alone in my single stall
measuring the elements
that foretell ovulation.

* *

I saw your face
in the electron microscope.
It was the frantic face
of the germ cell seeking life.

I saw my os
in the physician's glass.
It was eternity opening
its door a bit wider.

* * *

I wanted you in the biblical sense
as Deborah wanted Deborah.
I pitched my tent by the ocean,

I sang to the armies.
We brewed coffee and
sat all day in the water.
Then fishes circled me
in zebra stripes.

You held my hand.
Later we loved,
shades down.

Praise

I praise the invention of crackers
and sonograms
which turn the world
of sound to flesh.
I praise antacid
and the rocking chair
lovingly passed down.
I praise the monitor
which slides over jelly
and brings us our baby's heartbeat.

There is a needle which pierces
the great waters. I praise the piss
cultured in the lab.
It is the elixir of the heavens;
the blueprint of the soul.
I praise the womb.

I praise the feet and ankles and hips
and long white spine
braided like lanyard.
I praise the hand
that scratches
an ear and the mouth
that swallows fluid.

Let her keep turning in the world below.
Let her grow as you make me grow.

Little xx

There are orbs on strand g
making you a healthy child.
There are crosses marking
the colony of Cell #7.
They come from the unknown
donor, once Christian,
now nothing. Little xx,

I cried when they told me
I had a daughter.

5. Postscript

Dedication Postscript

For the daughter in me
accepting her father's violence.

For the father in me
accepting his daughter's silence.

For the mother in me
accepting her father's violence.

For the daughter in me
accepting her mother's silence.